Belle Laide

Poems

———

JOANNE DOMINIQUE DWYER

Sarabande Books
LOUISVILLE, KENTUCKY

Managing Editor
Sarabande Books, Inc.
2234 Dundee Road, Suite 200
Louisville, KY 40205

Library of Congress Cataloging-in-Publication Data

  Dwyer, Joanne Dominique.
  [Poems. Selections]
  Belle laide : poems / by Joanne Dominique Dwyer.
    pages cm
  ISBN 978 1-936747-55-9 (pbk. : alk. paper)
  I. Title.
  PS3604.W92B45 2013
  811'.6—dc23
                    2012046283

Cover image by Heidi Cost.
Cover and text design by Sarabande Books.

Manufactured in the United States of America.
This book is printed on acid-free paper.

Sarabande Books is a nonprofit literary organization.

The Kentucky Arts Council, the state arts agency, supports
Sarabande Books with state tax dollars and federal funding from
the National Endowment for the Arts.

For my parents: Helen Hurley & James Dwyer

For my children: Paige Dominique Young & August Joseph Young

Belle Laide: *French, meaning beautiful ugly.*

Contents

III

I

Ars Poetica, or-Keeper-of-the-Water

First my father *Killing Me Softly* with his Roberta Flack album.
Then my son *Killing Me Softly* with his Fugees CD.
On my shoulder a carcinoma that will eventually kill me—
will eat my flesh, as I eat yours.
I bit hard, sucked hard, not to mark you as my possession
as the rancher burns his ranch insignia into young calves—
but to try and ingest, to take in
that which cannot be eaten.
Outside my window the tiny clawed feet of birds
slip on the ice in the cement birdbath
like the elderly couple who have not skated in half a century.
The birds peck and peck, but the ice remains
an impenetrable obstacle to thirst.
I can see why lovers commit suicide together.
And why you enter me with such abandon—
a blind man's stick tap, tapping
resolved to the knowledge that death is always
only a foot in front of him. At any moment
the cane may fail him and he may fall
into the deepest, blackest well.
Excuse me *un momentito,* while I boil
water to pour on the ice. Bullshit!
you're not going to take time to boil water
when it scalds right from the tap.
I admire the couple for strapping
on those blades after all these years.
At least they have each other to hold onto.
And one can always drive the other to the hospital.

I feel like Charles Bukowski—
I eat small pork sausages with my hands,
wipe the grease on my pajamas
and speak about the opposite sex with scorn.
Though I doubt I'll ever be able to bare my soul
as uninhibited as he. Blame it on paralytic
poisons, the incarceration of consonants,
and the distraction of hundreds of birds
landed outside my window—
and my full time obsession
as keeper of their water.

Coat-of-Arms

Desire is not the root of all suffering,
though it's better to pull up the roots
of the weeds you desire to be rid of,
rather than poison them. For nothing
will grow again in that dirt.
I never read philosophy. It hurts
the way a fall from the monkey bars does,
or an argument with someone you desire
that goes round n' round and ends in a knock-out
or an even less satisfying temporary truce.
Birds keep getting stuck in the body of my stove.
I open the soapstone door and they surface
soot-covered, disoriented; battering
their tiny skulls against glass.
Eventually finding their way out
through one of the opened windows—
the way I want to find my way through to the verisimilar you
if there is such a thing, changing as we do
our passwords, our undergarments, the pets in our garages.
Desire cannot be the root of *all* suffering!
Hunger and loneliness or ineradicable pain perhaps.
The boa is hard-wired to crush endoskeletons.
Every religion has their saints and their power mongers.
Some are allergic to strawberries.
To be human *is* to desire.
Eggs and garlic and the oil of the evening primrose.
The pollen hurting some, others unaffected.
The only agreed upon creed: *Do no harm.*

I like to be under the canopy of trees,
so you could say I desire shade,
the heads of tiny quail in puff pastry
and my children to outlive me,
that I may give them my land.
The dome of the cerebellum an umbrella.
White paint is falling from the eaves of my roof.
Today I loaded a stack of old coats
into black garbage bags and left them
on a loading dock behind the Salvation Army—
unsure that the portal into the sky
will fit us all.

Harem

I don't get out much—socially, for adult pleasure.
     But I read a lot.
Most recently I read about Turkish Harems,
     learned the words: *odalisque, la belle esclave.*
I learned that having hair on one's private parts
     was considered a sin
and the enslaved women whitened their faces
     with the pulp of almonds and jasmine.
I drive my daughter to her ceramics class
     where not only do I admire her hands in red clay,
but also the muscled arms of her female teacher.
     At the harem baths women inspected each other intimately,
scanning skin for signs of new growth. When needed,
     a burning paste of peppered honey was applied and then scraped
with the shell of a blue-lipped mussel, removing hair and follicle.
     I learned that castrated men stood guard over the harem;
sometimes the women took these beardless men as lovers.
     And even after silverware was introduced into the harem,
around 1830, the women preferred their hands, maintaining
     that taste is transmitted through the fingertips.
I learned the Koran allowed each man four wives
     and as many female slaves as he could afford.
The average age in a harem was seventeen.
     Opium was ingested nightly
causing insomnia, then fitful dreams of lost homelands—
     amnesia when the sun rose.
My ex-husband used to warn me
     about the dangers of being alone with my imagination.

In a night of madness Ibrahim Sultan had his entire harem
    put inside sacks and drowned.
I learned that the color of the harem women's *mendils*
    (handkerchiefs) conveyed unspoken messages:
blue signified hope for union, black bleakness and separation.
    And the dream I had two nights ago
of a bald and naked woman rising
    from the azure-tiled water of a swimming pool
is making sense to me:
    The water removed the veil.
And last night, I dreamt of the transference of crushed shell
    into my mouth, delivered by a stranger's lips.
I bought a Persian Cold Wax Hair Removal kit from the
    health food store, and last month I went to a wedding.
I sat at a table with an electrician and his wife
    and a single man who had been to prison for drugs.
Perhaps because I don't get out much, and because
    I am obsessed with a fear of jails,
I asked the single man for jail stories.
    Imagine this: You are locked in a room
with seventy or so other prisoners sleeping on cots.
    Five or six men surround a single cot and swaddle an inmate in a grey
      blanket,
then punch and kick and head-bang him into unconsciousness.
    The victim's cries are muted, and the assailants' fists unmarked.
And you don't dare to rise from your cot in protest, or defense—
    Instead you feign sleep.
The electrician's wife became uncomfortable

and changed the topic of conversation to plastic surgery:
Her sister is married to a plastic surgeon in Dallas,
    whose specialty is facelifts.
The sister had a breast job done by her husband's friend.
    The deluxe wife-of-a-doctor-job entailed
the removal of each nipple, the insertion of implants, then the sewing up
    of slit skin and the return of the nipples.
Unfortunately, the nipples no longer match-up horizontally.
    But what I have trouble vacating from my mind
is the vision of two severed areolas lying disembodied
    on a table of surgical steel, left marked from right,
submerged in a saline solution, waiting.
    I suppose razors were not safe
in the hands of harem women.
    It is said that Mohammed had altruistic motives
when sanctioning polygamy—envisioning it
    as a solution to female infanticide.
All of my daughter's pots come out of the kiln
    unbroken and hair flowers on her in new places,
coaxed by the lengthening days.
    Like I said I don't get out much,
but there are no prison guards or eunuchs
    standing at my door, preventing my exit.
Nor a secret lover awaiting a sign
    from the color of the scarf circling my neck.
I have yet to use the hair removal kit
    as the instructions warn: *the skin must be free of oil and dirt.*

Late Night Confessions

I met a man last night who is afraid of dogs.
He said, *In Sweden pit bulls are outlawed.*
We built a fire from dead yucca
and talked about the selective biting habits of domestic felines:
his cat attacks some women, but not others.
We talked of mimicry: the mimicry of the oppressor
to copy the style of the oppressed.
The female tiger butterfly mimics the monarch,
replicates its wing design and sun colors
without ever having to feed on poison milkweed.
But he was referring to Hip Hop artists
and women forced to veil themselves.

The man who is afraid of dogs, his girlfriend, and I
go out into the cold night air to collect more yucca.
The girlfriend says to no one in particular
that her shampoo contains yucca
and that her eyes itch, but she cannot cry.
I tell them St John's Wort has done nothing for me.
I don't tell them about the dream I had of my children
burning inside a small hut.

The man who is afraid of dogs
lives just below the Arctic Circle where
for three months of winter the air is black,
without sun. He wants to know why we Americans
are consumed with the history of other cultures
and not our own. He wants to know why in New Mexico

there are so many crosses on the sides of our roads
and so many churches without bells.
I tell him horny toads are endangered.
I don't tell him about the miracle staircase.

I confess to the Swede that I too am afraid of pit bulls—
I'm afraid of the type of people who own pit bulls.
I don't tell him about my non-violent lesbian
friend who owns a pit bull named Sugar
and that I have put my hands inside the dog's mouth.
I don't tell him about my Chilean painter friend who
in his younger years backpacked through Europe.
He liked Sweden very well, with fond memories
of being in bed with a woman and her mother.
Or should I say a woman and her daughter?

As the flames of the fire geld,
the man who is afraid of dogs
asks where my husband is.
He calls me a grass widow,
but does not solicit
whether it's war or famine.
I imagine myself mimicking a faithful wife
standing on the shore, gazing out to sea
yearning for the return of my seafaring husband.
But the truth is: I don't stand on the shore often.
I get in the water, and I like the water bracing
and the waves hurricane high.

Barely a Body Comes Knocking

Barely a body comes knocking
Too many holes in the road to get here
Muss up your fancy car
All the women on TV with hair extensions
Making all us other women feel low-grade
And a little lying-down sequacious
So we buy more red dye #3 candy and clown accessories

Barely a shoe comes imprinting the earth
Barely a census-taker in a white hat
Barely a beggar
And if you come to steal eggs or ice skates
My chickens will peck out your eyes

And my assistant ghosts will hex your virility
And you will sit all your remaining days
In a rocking chair like a ceramic troll on the porch
Of the state home in Maine for old and demented alcoholic ship builders
Because the home for old and alcoholic sailors is full

You think I'm semiserious
I do my best work when hypnopompic
Half awake, half asleep
Half-cultivated, half-composted
My dress on inside out

Barely a delivery driver comes
Barely a sexually repressed Jehovah Witness wearing a cheap suit

Barely a peloton of bike racers
Long gone are the days when a wagon full of a family going West
Would approach the perimeter of shade and ask for salt
Even a longer expanse has elapsed since a man on a horse
Would be obliged for some water from the pump near to the pigpen
But first to stick his head under the effluxing spout

Barely a body comes knocking
And when you get old they take your driver's license away
As if to explain the language error or the ill behavior
Not an encyclopedia salesman
Nor a neighbor asking to borrow your yellow plates

Aphonic

I write so I don't have to speak.
—Tadeusz Rozewicz

I place my body on the bus from the airport
of palm fronds and men holding up placards
routing north away from pavement towards soil
in the direction of trees whose limbs labor papaya and avocado,
towards small edifices of concrete block painted
watermelon pink and the tones of semiprecious stones.
The sea a place you could lose your daughter in—
envelop or swallow or seize or cease to exist.
On the night plaza a vespertine and diminutive girl
with a broad-boned face and black penumbra bangs
almost curtaining her coal-colored eyes.
Dark as I imagine the bottom of a diamond mine,
shoe-polished and nested in a nighthawk's aerie.
She tells me her name, *Mimi,* but can't tell me her age,
even when I ask in fingers.
She shows me her miniature animals,
placing one at a time into the platform of my palm.
I name them as best as I can:
Animals of the farm: *Vaca, caballo, puerco.*
Animals of the jungle: *Elefante, jirafa, tigre.*
Not long ago I heard one of the twin poets
read a poem about God being white
and I couldn't tell if he meant that as a good or a bad thing.
As in lucent and shining white light God
or as in white supremacist go to the supermarket
for liverwurst and other vacuum packed lunch meats God.
Though he equated his incapacitating migraines with white,
I still could not decipher his intent.

My missing daughter returned by midday muted,
having been held on a rooftop.
And the gelded leather-skinned cobbler hammering shoes
sprawled on the grey ground of stone in the twilit plaza
while the children twirl and partner dance
in their florid prince and princesa costumes
is without legs below his knees.
A footless repairer of huaraches and boots
and white plastic communion shoes that need resoling.

Surrender

To be baptized is to surrender—
to let that long-haired honey cradle you
as if you were a queen, or a prostitute,
or the girl I see at the city pool
who cannot lift herself and is therefore lifted
from her wheelchair, set afloat in a pink tube
like wet laundry waiting to be hung in the sun.
Does the man waiting to be executed
fear death more because he was never baptized?
As if the river could swallow our sins
and keep them secret.
As if algae-green water lapping
over the foreheads of molting snakes
could convert their venom into a cerulean cure for madness.
As if buckets or ladles of blessed water
poured over the heads of infants and small-clawed otters
could safeguard them from stampede.
Submerging my head into, and drinking from,
a birdbath, a horse trough,—a squirt gun shot
into the mouth of the girl in the pool,
a high-powered hose scouring the prison cell
and the man balled-up in the corner
looking like Picasso's *Crouching Beggar*
or *Woman Huddled on the Ground with a Child*
painted from the penciled sketches he made
in the women's prison in Paris,
where nuns doubled as guards
and children were confined in cells with their mothers.

Hose *me* down, and up, into cavities and crevices—
any place I might be hiding.
Be it a full submergence:
The waterfall under which we stuttered,
or the *cenotes* in the Yucatan
where we jumped from the graffiti-tagged cliffs
and swam in the aphotic black water.
Be it a full submergence:
The mother held all five of her children
down—one at a time in the bathtub.
Same rationale as the priest:
to save them from Satan.
Only she didn't let them back up.
Only it was no longer a braided river.
Paul shat in the water.
Luke wanted his rubber duck.
John bit her finger.
Mary spoke her first word underwater.
Noah struggled, still in his pajamas—
reaching for the plug.

Feral Fields

Days of nausea—as if I were on a boat,
newly pregnant or terribly ashamed.
Days of rain in the desert, the sun asleep
and my nipples sore, as if they were being sucked
by eighteen newborn piglets, or chafed
by a dress made from burlap sacks—
or the horsehair robe of a monk.
That monk wants it as much as any man does.
And weeds I've never seen before
bloom into purple, orange and yellow-headed
flowers smelling of the mice
fetuses I found in my daughter's boots—
a daughter who no longer lives here.
It's deceiving, with the car windows rolled up
the fields of *aster, charlock* and *agoseris*
appear soothing and odorless.
Magritte's painting of a girl
in a black & white pinafore
tearing apart a meadowlark with her teeth
is titled *Le plaisir.*
The priest had no trouble feeling
entitled to his, nor me to mine—
be it dark chocolate, or an injured man.
I sent off the boots, having let them air in the sun,
having banged them on the flagstone floor—
wanting to empty and make disappear
every last fragment of bone, remnant of fur,
of aorta, of hind tendon from the nest.

I can hear the squirrels living in my walls
scratching their fleas—or are they fucking?
The flowers only beautiful from a distance.
I want it as much as any woman does.
Asking neither forgiveness, nor affection,
perhaps a little something to settle the bile,
to ease the feral ferocity for flesh—
be it a pound or a casket-full.

Under House Arrest

1.

As we walk unveiled in sunlight
at midday with pairs of sharp scissors in our hands
out to cut the dahlias before a freeze,
filling tubs with water for the lingering birds,
fertilizing our apricot trees,
taking our cars to the carwash,
buying lentils and chickpeas in cans from Whole Foods.
As we dance in sheer or opaque dresses
under fluorescent or new moons,
our legs tanned, our fingers manicured,
our children at home with babysitters
eating bowls of Franken Berry cereal.
As we go to dentists, to astrologers, to divorce attorneys,
as we go to the gym and to mammogram appointments
and to animal shelters and ice skating rinks
and King Sunny Ade concerts,
and have our furniture reupholstered,
our hips replaced—

Women in Afghanistan
are tired of house arrest,
tired of dress codes, prohibition of perfume.
They're tired of censorship, tired of the stoning,
tired of sex with men who collaborate.
They are tired of obedience—
tired of holding matchsticks to a flame,
darkening the rims of their eyes with the soot—

•

As we polish our grandmothers' silver sets,
bend to wipe the blood of our parakeets
from the Persian rugs in our bedrooms,
as we cover our hands in mink mittens
when the electricity goes out during an ice storm
or yellow plastic gloves when we accidentally
break the thermometer and are afraid
of the mercury on the rim of the bathtub.
As we see the woman wobbling
near the dumpster behind Pizza Hut
with a bruise under her eye, as we battle insomnia
and sun spots, and notch crooked marks
on our own mauve-plastered walls—

Women of Afghanistan
are tired of losing teeth, the blackened windows,
the looks on their daughters' faces—
They are tired of the snow and of bathing
and the knowledge that
arms held up to protect oneself
from a crowd throwing stones
soon becomes a meaningless gesture.

2.
The crime is her breast; the crime is her eyes.
The crime is her cunt; the crime is her hair.

•

The crime is her breast, a perpetual field
of opium, more for the child than the man—
It reminds him of his thirst.

The crime is her eyes, cat eyes in the dark,
small hardened pears, wild hazelnuts watching
men leave, locking doors behind them.

The crime is her cunt, the one fertile valley
in a dry landscape of clenched fists and scaly thumbs
that reminds men of nomadic tents strewn in black hides.

The crime is her hair. Oiled tresses hold the forbidden scent of jasmine,
remind men of the manes of untamed ponies,
the furs of endangered animals.
Women can weave spells into their hair
and a man could find his fingers tangled in a woman's hair—
never wanting to leave, walking behind her.

Photuris P.

The light that shines from a firefly is chemical:
luciferin and *luciferase*. A pigment and an enzyme.

They depend on each other. Neither one can produce a luminous body alone.
Even the arrival of the average child requires both the sperm and the egg.

A man and a woman in love is always the preferred choice for entry.
But sometimes one accepts a misandrist mother and an anonymous vial of sperm.

Or an angel, gray-winged, timing its appearance with the arrival of dawn,
or the dismissal of dusk, wearing a foreign, yet familiar fragrance.

Immaculada was the name given to the girl-child born out of wedlock.
(The removal of rust by the sheer power of the wind.)

To make immune: from the draft, from the disease, from the theory of love.
To impale the innocent, accused of nothing more than stealing.

Could you make a list of every object you have stolen?
A blue sweater, a bedpan, a sandpiper skull,

two snow tires, a lifejacket, a deck of pornographic playing cards,
fireflies from my brother's jar and his ponyskin jacket.

Lucifer: did he free-fall, or was he pushed? Or was there a fault in design—
a missing enzyme? (A flower-covered coffin for the fallen angel.)

•

Children go into the night carrying glass jars with air holes punched into the lids.
A random run, imagined flight, cupping light into the cave of two hands.

On the seventh floor, in the highest heaven, the place where God is said to reside,
the oxygen content of the air is too low to sustain a fire *or* a life.

And children sleep with the insects held captive on their bedside tables:
a small array of constellations moving through a diminished air.

Bears and Marmots

> The poet is he that hath fat enough, like bears and marmots,
> to suck his claws all winter. He hibernates in this world and
> feeds on his own marrow.   —Henry David Thoreau

In the news there is a yogi in orange from India
wearing beads said to be Shiva's tears
who says he has not eaten in 70 years
and it does not matter if he is lying.
I love him, regardless.
And whether you have high
or low cholesterol, tie your shoelaces or not,
The Song Remains the Same. Sometimes
there are no doors, but a set of hanging beads,
a rollercoaster in another city. The military
kept him under observation for 15 days
hoping for clues as to how soldiers might
survive while deprived of food and water
and concluded *we cannot shut our eyes
to possibilities, to a source of energy other than calories.*
And I shut my eyes. Eat every few hours.
Graze like a child in the back of a bakery
or livestock let loose in the mountains.
You are more of an ascetic surviving
on the fruit in your orchard, the frozen bones
in your freezer. Thoreau was a vegetarian
who ate moose. My mother once stole
a can of tuna fish. And I shut my eyes.
People who are obsessed with woodchucks
and marmots are called *marmotophiles.*
I step on the scale most mornings
as if a number might hold meaning.

I am eating a bushel of blueberries as we speak,
three loaves of bread.
Better to sit with a scissor and sew a cape—
hold the lid of a garbage can to the sky.
The yogi said *at a young age*
I was set apart by a goddess.
Once released, he refuses a ride in the armored car.
Walking barefoot back to his village he senses
sap ascending a thicket of teak—
the unsullied sun on the nape of his neck.

Notes on Photuris P.

1

the lamp which is the light from the insect—
a color and a catalyst
we called them lightening bugs—
soft-bodied, nocturnal

2

what mother could make audible
the proclamation that her child
is average?

3

or a man alone
with an omnivorous womb

4

beware of the man who disguises
or disposes of his scent

5

Immaculada is a Flamenco dancer
whose father denies her existence—
whose stepfather refused to walk her down the aisle.
She dances each night
as if they were / were not in the audience

6

the crime is in the gluttony, in the having too much
not in those chapped hands reaching
for the pie in the windowsill

7

Magnificent Angel with your scraped knees . . .

Angel's request:

confess

8

how did we arrive at the parking lot of a convent—

did those nuns pray for us:

the thieves of snow tires?

the cards were hidden from his wife
in the back corner of his closet—

policeman: Harlem, homicide.
one summer afternoon, we broke into his home
and drank pink lemonade

I had the pony—
until my legs lengthened beyond her belly

9

the handsomest of the four sons
left his testicles on top of his mother's dresser
he was a sculptor, first
I visited him in the State Hospital
he was wearing a white gown, sitting up in bed
hair like the shining tail of a horse
washed and combed by a girl

eyes like almonds
bled to death in a winter stream

10

fear of enclosure, of straps, of paper

11

fear of elevators

12

net, dove, dark

if an owl is colorblind

if an owl is colorblind, then of course the French
must name their straightjackets *camisoles de force.*
And regardless of whether Jesus was the son of a god,
or the son of a man, he must have practiced *coitus
interruptus,* or at least spread honey on his member.
And if he had impregnated a lover he would have read her
Persian poems and used his carpenter's tools to craft a cradle.

Do you remember the tiny old woman who lived behind
the post office, the diabetic we drank tequila with—
the one who never learned to read, but told us stories
of being married at thirteen to a man who broke
her collarbone, whose first two children did not live
long enough to taste solid food—
the one who would beg us to dance with her
on her linoleum floor to Kris Kristofferson's *Me and Bobby McGee*
played over and over again on her portable record player?

How I miss the scent of limes, the sun exiting so early,
the ambulance arriving after the tequila & the two-stepping.
And us watching from our apartment window with the snow
plummeting as she was wheeled out in blankets and belted.
Our apartment that lay on top of the town's one grocery store
which we broke into one night through the basement window
and stole two loaves of bread and a bag of dog food.

How I miss the geometry of eclipses, the lifestyle
of a part-time thief, the time to dance with a neighbor.

Do you remember the picture of Jesus that hung
on her kitchen wall - his heart an exposed flame
that burned like a limerent wound, like a falling sun?
His eyes shaded with a sadness that made you want
to play *Bobby McGee* for him, to dance close enough
to taste him, to whisper in his ear that you
are intrigued by his nickname: *little lamb.*
Chop, puppet, thorn.

The Relativity of Sorrow

Mercy is the combing of tangled hair
the sewing up of a split lip
the *staying* of an execution.
So the prisoner remains alive
until he or she dies a *natural* death
and the priest returns to say the last rites
one more time like an encore
of rednecks shouting *Freebird*.
Mercy, Mercy Me sang Marvin Gaye,
but he was shot in the head anyway.
Thomas Hardy only wrote love poems
to his wife after her death. When she lived,
she lived in the attic, closer to the clouds.
Domesticated is such a risk: a false wall,
toothpick fence, the mute swan in the playpen.
Grandpa reading dirty magazines in the outhouse
near to fields of melon and corn
and lynchings in July with blue snow cones.
Or the days of just take the thief down
to the chopping block.
Mercy seat is the resting place of God.
On the Sabbath he sits in the lap of a loving infidel.
When forgiven a heart fractures
into fallow fragments of birdshot.
Having arrived after the hunter,
Tess of the D'Urbervilles
broke the necks of the injured pheasants.
Mercy is the sap of pine,

popsicle sticks stacked to make a palace.
Reading and re-reading the *Runaway Bunny*
when you'd rather be exfoliating or shopping online.
Mercy is sometimes the smothering with a pillow,
or kindness to an ex. Compared
in some ancient text to a sword.

In the Arms of Morpheus

The world's first morphine addict was the wife
of the man who invented the hypodermic needle
and birds practice their song patterns
by singing in their dreams.
I have a singer-songwriter friend whose latest job
is driving around Northern New Mexico in a van
distributing needles to addicts.
She herself suffers from sessions of darkness
that escort her to bottles of any genre of alcohol.
And every night you trim your nails, sweep the clippings
with the karate chop part of your hand
along the mock marble of your vanity
into an un-lidded jam jar—apple or maybe apricot.
So many people are contracting Hepatitis C or getting married.
In one dream an obsidian-haired woman
removed all the clothes from my closet.
In another I am the desired prey of a brutal black wolf.
In order to survive the aftermath of God's wrath
I would behead a pregnant frog
or tenderly care for her eggs,
though I'm in favor of the sky to simmer down.
The fortune cookie yesterday:
No man is free unless he is master of himself.
The men and women approaching the van
scratching their throats. The somniliquy
of sounding out untamed words in the dark.
The needle inventor's wife was also the first
to die of a narcotic overdose.

In last night's wedding dream
I wore an haute couture white gown.
But hidden underneath the scabbard of silk
were Vibram-soled knee-high brown leather boots
that got me safely through the snow
and the ice of the unplowed parking lot
and to the reception held in another building.

Discalced

Forgive me, St. Teresa of Avila—
There are enough pairs of shoes in my closet
    to shod a homeless shelter or a small orphanage.
You who founded an order of nuns
    clad in hand-woven sandals of rope,
you who scarred your own flesh.
    There's a virus transmitted from a man
that scars mine. When they exhumed your body
    a perforation was found in your left ventricle,
legitimizing the story you told about an angel
    spearing a lance into your entrails.
It's unlikely I will ever need
    to spear a fish or a bison for food.
Cannibals aren't always blood-thirsty—
    sometimes it's an attachment disorder,
like nettles clinging to undergarments,
    or a crane on the back of a cow.
It's even less likely that I will ever transpose
    my love for a man to God,
though I put knives into people in my dreams
    and it rains white and scarlet.
You titled your treatise *The Interior Castle*
    and I imagine you penitently regal
behind cold stone eating the stomachs of sheep
    espousing your soul to His like a swallowtail
leveled between parchment
    or a mail-order bride aboard a steamer with her trunk.

Before you entered the convent
        you had an illicit love affair
that ended badly
        and today in a cathedral in Spain
your incorrupt right foot is on display behind glass.
        Elsewhere a finger from your right hand,
your left eye, a fragment of your jaw
        and your flagellation cord.
I want to give you my rust-red
        sling-back high heels. And sit on a stool
like a shoe salesman and hold your feet in my hands,
        fasten the straps around your chilblained ankles,
rub the oil of oranges into your calves.
        St. Teresa, today is Good Friday, 2009
and the sky is a dominant dome.
        Forgive me for the stories I tell to atone.
I am a saintless voyeur sitting
        on an aluminum roof in the sun
reading about you,
        and about the reproductive hazards of insects.
The way the male grips the female's
        abdomen for hours.

II

The Skin of an Otter

If to love is to imagine
let me imagine a red thread
exiting the windpipe of a ghost.
That I may suture my veins to yours,
sew up the hem of the doll's ragged collar.
That I may embroider the wings of black flies
into the lashes of your walnut-shelled eyes.
If to love is to imagine
let me imagine the human spine as a ladder.
That I might climb up your bent back,
keep the birds from your hair—
replace the burnt bulbs in the ceiling.
There are war crimes in all of our museums,
fences topped with broken bottles and barbed crowns,
the remains of shattered furniture in the sacked city.
If to love is to imagine, let me imagine
an adulation as intact as the skin of an otter,
as laden as Aphrodite's uterus
carrying the fetuses of seven daemons.
The tongues of the trees Pentecostal in their singing.
The ear never the same after the dove.

I Draw Blood

I draw blood from your lip
as if I were a bird.
That I might levitate, that I might land.
I've pulled up all the rugs.
I want harder surfaces.
Standing barefoot at the kitchen stove
you encircle me from behind.
Cloak me like a cloth over a birdcage.
Kissing my neck at the carotid artery,
I am broken down into filaments of aluminum,
reduced to the drip of a faulty faucet.
I fight the dog for a bone. Alone
I see beauty in the sunlight
refracted in the hairs on my arm.
Feel like banging my head—
against what?
Walls are beautiful.
Flying buttresses keep the demons from descending.
I took my first confession in twenty-four years
in the cathedral of Notre Dame.
The stained-glass saints pallid below the rose window.
I was crying so much the 83 year old priest who spoke six languages
asked if I was a murderess—
yet assigned me no penance.
Saint Patrick was a runaway slave
whose faith grew in captivity.
To levitate is to let go the safety of land
and shopping carts and check-points.

One summer night at a seaside amusement park—
stench of beer and lemon pepper on corn,
cotton candy and vomit, hermit crabs
and sandpipers hiding from the floodlights in the sand.
My father and I on the crown of the Ferris wheel
when the cage came unlocked.
His arms grasping me in—
trying to forfend my fall.

Animal Love

It seems like an angel
delivered him into your arms,
but you held him at arm's-length
so he cut off your arms
to be near to you.
It seems like an angel
brought you together, illuminating him
with a cop's flashlight in the dim bar.
Shining the light from his eyes
to his feet, he has a slight gap in his teeth.
If you asked for mercy
you got the cracked claws of brown bears
and the severed clitorises of seven snow leopards
boiled down into a poultice
and applied everywhere it hurt.
He raises sheep, but won't let you see them,
has dogs that do not bark.
And a scar where they cut
into his heart as a boy.
As a boy, as a buoy. Hold on.
So it seems like an angel carried him piggyback
and he spared her his spurs,
yet neither one of us dares to dream of flight.
Only dead skin and the fin of a shark.
Hold on. There's no heat in the house
and the sun is growing weak.
I mix a little aphrodisiac
into the birdseed, so more birds

will come to my house than yours.
It's lonely at the top. I rule my world.
Spitting into rusted coffee cans,
whistling the mating calls of white sparrows.
It's lonely at the bottom—
like a mudsucker gliding along
swishing its tail, filtering through
all that settles on the pond floor
into its mouth,
but swallowing little.

Absolution

I was once slapped at the bottom of a staircase
by a woman who gave me her DNA,
punched against a breezeway wall
by a man in a denim jacket I embroidered.
If love is a door—
let's unhinge its plumb in the vertical plane,
fell it all over again with a crosscut saw,
lie in the open air on its cellulose surface
under a quilt made with the pelage of milkweed pods—
and ask the stars for absolution.
Orion was a stud hunter,
he was also god of the flea people.
All five of his wives ran off itchy.
See the yellow forsythia swaying in the wind;
the death of the horses in the fire.
There is a trance inducing technique
where you bang your head
against a door of rabbit pelts.
Another involves staring at the orgy
of bodies ablaze inside the sun.
You stained and hung the door between
my son's room and the magenta wall.
Your hand coaxed me down the mountain—
a hand on an iron lever, a hand on an oar.
Three captive bodies dangle
from the tooled leather at Orion's waist
and Job asked *Can we not loosen the belt of Orion?*
Like the surgeons on the Discovery channel trying to coerce

the Filipino man, who has lived for 54 years with the leg
of his unborn twin protruding from his stomach,
to let them amputate.
In the darkness of his interior
teeth and hair and the tiny bones
of his twin's pelvis lodged near his spleen.
His wife feeling polygamous
each time she feeds him rice.
If love is a door—
the back entrance to a cave,
leave a tinplate of polyfloral honey
and the rinds of limes on the threshold.
See the termites devouring oak.

The Last Shepherd Down

Perhaps there is another type of writing, I only know this
one: in the night, when fear does not let me sleep.
—Franz Kafka

You once told me the last shepherd down
from the mountain sets fire to the mountain.
Having lived as a child near to Navajos, you know.
I feel disgrace in the dirt under my fingernails,
in the cyst in my arm like a small gopher hill,
in the crack in the stone of my forehead
formed from the way I sleep on my belly
having lived near to loud speakers.
One Sunday we set fire to the pyre
of brush we piled in your pasture.
You with the gasoline and the rake;
me with the saw, ready spit on my lips.
The lambs locked down behind the gate,
the dog with ticks on her belly in the backyard.
Scratches like a bride's henna on the undersides of my arms,
both of us rasping ashes from our eyes.
I feel disgraced by my flawed ascension,
the way I never go home.
5–7 small white eggs in a shallow saucer of grass
in a drainpipe signifies a tiny-hooked swallow.
The word hormone introduced in 1902.
3 buff-brown eggs with black markings
in a nest lined with sticks and seaweed:
a black gull. And late last night
alcohol banished some blood-brain barrier,
made solvent some neurotransmitter,
and you share with me your almost unbearable

envy of a woman's body, which leads
to the eviction from our mouths the anguish
we have kept caged beneath our tongues
over our unborn children.
Last Shepherd, never stop rataplanning language in the dark—
the plastic arm of an action figure
is amputating in the flames.
I hate the word *whore*.
It's true what they say: my socialization is incomplete.
I will wear three birds' nests to my father's funeral,
candy corn in my teeth to my mother's.
I'm lying of course, but that's what we do—
wearers of headdresses, herders of words.
Last Shepherd, there's an abandoned beehive in my gut,
an autumn meadow waiting for rain.
Return to me with your bedding,
skin smelling of petroleum-soaked clover.
I have a bucket of warm milk in a wheelbarrow.

Beaded Baby Moccasins

If love is like a doll's shoe—
the color of nascent snow
that laces over the ankle
or the polychromatic beaded baby moccasins
we saw lying in the museum drawer
that belonged to an infant from a sea tribe of seal hunters.
Or the rutilant pink blossoms
of the locust tree that bloomed in the dark
while I slept dreaming of my arrival on a red-eye
wearing a long-to-the-floor skirt—
not of a postulant, but of a flower vendor
or a woman covering disfigurement.
Freud believed religious faith
a wish-fulfilling illusion.
I can't locate faith in a carved or uncarved pew.
I'm more focused on the altar boy's shoes.
Under his rope-tied white robe
he's wearing a man's black loafers
desolately oversized for his small feet
with sufficient spare space for a coyote den in each toe.
I want to buy him a kite.
If love is a mezzanine floor we might not fall from,
a hand holding back my hair from my face
as I'm sick on the side of the bus.
The mouth so at home in the vicinity of pavement.
Pew also means to enclose, as in *men who were*
as willingly pewed in the parish church
as their sheep were in night folds.

Freud also believed civilized life imposes suffering,
yet he always wore a dinner jacket.
We delaminate layers of old paint,
bleach sheets in the shielded shade.
I separate out the oily ham from the beans,
the unflattering photos from the folio
and the quotes about repressed homosexuality
being the reason Sigmund's patient "Little Hans"
is afraid of horses.

Supine in the Sun in the Neighborhood of Naked

> You must stay drunk on writing so reality
> cannot destroy you.   —Ray Bradbury

I am supine in the sun in the neighborhood of naked,
meaning I have a kite in my lap, strata of black loam
on my cheek. If the creek will let me sleep near to it

I won't have to hoist myself up onto the counter
to reach the cabinet where the sugar is housed.
Meaning you shoved me down the elevator shaft,

and I still want to crawl up inside you, lay my last eggs.
Meaning you are furred in the small of your back
and in the place where your head is assigned to your body.

The junction where women sing as they clothes-pin.
Near to the water tower, near to the train depot.
The junction where we rupture through the roadblock

giddy-upping on horse-on-a-sticks.
Human beings must love something, and,
in the dearth of worthier objects of affection

will love a horse-on-a-stick.
The way as a child Jane Eyre had nothing to love
but a doll—could not sleep without that doll.

Meaning I don't watch the news, because I don't want to know.
I could swim until I could no more.
Good thing you were already acquainted with Resuscitation Annie,

•

so you knew just how to blow into my mouth, pound on my chest.
In Spain we swam in the sea and I wrapped my legs around your waist
and it scared you as if I were a cinderblock.

Meaning, I only want to practice idolatry of the orange moon
and of a man whose stitching is separating, not because he was sewn
in a sweat shop, but because he was left in a sandbox in the rain.

Meaning *inebriation* is a beautiful word.

Possession

I am making my way from one un-landscaped yard to another
wearing short-shorts and thin-soled sandals.
There is a baby on my hip,
a chestnut-colored fox is following
trying to bite the baby and my leg.
Then a beehive in a closet top shelf,
my fingers like primitive tools
attempting to pull flattened flowers
from the sheaf without agitating the swarm.
All grey matter like compressed paper pulp.
The baby spoke words like an animistic oracle
whose stomach is sated with plums
and the hand-milked milk of mountain goats.
I keep looking for signs that you love someone else.
I said *careful of the bees.*
I am without the protective suit.
It was St. Augustine who incited
the terrible campaign against Eve.
The man who once said
Lord, give me chastity, but not yet.
Today's new word: abreaction.
It may not appear alluring at first,
but it is followed
by *abreast, abri* and *abridge.*
To shelter oneself in the cavity of a hillside,
side by side in the sun.
In bed we flip through an architectural
magazine. You linger on a spread

about a rich white woman named Tonia
who has a Japanese-styled room in her home
for her Zen tea ceremonies. Photographed
in contemplation in full kimono regalia,
her robe and her skin are the color
of achromatic sheetrock.
You are intrigued with her
and I hate her.

Wedded to Dirt

If to love is to fall,
then I'm flat out.
Knee-down on the cement handicap ramp,
slammed fetal near the dog bowl
on the poppy-red linoleum.
In the moonlit field of alfalfa and iris
I am wedded to dirt, to the imprint of body.
See me fainting in St. Augustine's arms,
or lying low in a canoe on the river of Lethe.
A water leak in the bark,
claret spittle on the corners my mouth.

If to love is to fall
find me in the root cellar
drinking Milk of Magnesia with Billie Holiday.
She's in a half-slip and a pointed bra,
swaying on tiptoes standing on a crate of soda bottles
beneath the window
trying to catch a little light
from the constellation of Venus.
I'm lying under old newspapers
drenched from night sweats—
not wanting to tell her there's a ladder.

Request to a Lover

Sometimes it is so dark
I have to rely on the other senses.
Or eat the black licorice or shredded tires.
No window, or light, in the oven—
one must smell the scent
of rabbit and cow colliding.
Your hand fluttering towards
the touch-sensitive lamp on the bedside table.
It hurts when your head hits mine,
the temple being so vulnerable
to sacking, to pharaoh ants, to new beliefs
on sanity and sacrificial virgins.
Run now, while there is still light!
While grandma is still grandma,
and not the wolf. Sink my battleship
before I sink yours. Yet,
the prayer remains the same:
Do not maim. O half-bitten tongue!
We stole sun-warm cherries from a tree
in the abandoned orchard outside of Granada
and watched a halter-less horse
grazing wild grass near a stone wall.
Solitude in the white darkness.
Don't make me see!
Loosen my ligaments a little,
comb my hair. There are new ways
of looking at Judas Iscariot
or a woman with plumber's crack.

In the Louvre we saw the carved bit of ass
showing on the Venus of Milo.
Lift my dressing gown over my head,
or take it all the way down.
Look me in the eye when we make love
so I don't mistake you for a blind man.
Don't be afraid of my dark,
buy me a bird of my own—
spit on the candle in the corner.

Bareback

Another meaning of ghost
is mask, and my feet are cold
on the pine floor in the thin socks
I have been wearing for three days running,
meaning consecutive, meaning *disembodied*
spirit. Meaning I prefer the newer blue masking
tape over the standard oat brown.
Uneasy at the thought of that tape
tangled and twisted inside me
like the nausea I had last night watching
my seventeen-year-old goddaughter
push out her baby.
I am weaning out the illusions of love.
Caravaggio's cupid is asleep on the cold ground.
The old black dog is asleep on the flea-seeped sofa.
Duct tape seals the cracks in the door to keep out
the wind that I love more than most people.
The wind in turn loving lilac bushes and foxes more than me.
Are love's tragedies predestined?
The pulverized flesh of a dried red chili pod
on the bathmat, a little blood on my slip,
aioli on his slacks, milk on the magpie's lips.
Should we spot treat the stain before it appears
and leave the sack to soak in the Laundromat
where the woman who mops the floor
is in love with the floor?
Hieronymus painted a small man hugging a huge owl.
It looked like neither one would ever hurt the other.

Love rides bareback on longing—
knees get skinned, shins scabbed.
Potion so close to poison.
I'm sliding my way to the basement.
The bee keeper's mask is made of metal and mesh.
We can be *God* or *Satan* for Halloween,
give up *liquids* or *love* for Lent.
Hurry! We can still get tickets to the tent
where the candy-stained mouth of the prophet
is lying on a platform of plywood
with beautiful bruises on her hips.

In the Geometry of Less

If love is to hurt
hurt me in the geometry of less.
Wet place in the grass of the kitten's piss.
In the diameter of a currant.
In the dimensions of a doll house.
Where the poison laid upon the strands of grass
is judicious and juices the jagged thirst of an ant
and the angles of the sun
come in the tiny cellophane window
and prism light onto the pale
hardened legs of a plastic woman
and a man whose body is the length of a frail lizard.
Your body is not the weapon, but the weeping
contained on a lawn chair in the dark.
I've never seen anyone devour so deftly
a whole orange rind before,
nor torch such high temperature from the tongue.
If love is to hurt
let it be in the increments of an ascending ladder
that leans towards the shaded side of such a sky
as El Greco painted shirtless in winter.
You shamed me for that one lift of my dress.
Scarlet slap of pigment in the pines,
a nail in my foot all those years ago.
Such traversed-upon skin
blistered from the brush of a leaf.
Against such vulnerability we collide.

Kyphosis

If love is housed in the shucked pea part of the brain
called the pituitary gland,
atop a tiny bone known as the Turkish saddle.
As if the placement of a limp-limbed body
lashed to the leather were a message to the enemy.
Even Thumbelina would hit her head on the ceiling.
I want your hands on my temple.
Incense or no incense.
Old women walking to the well with curves in their spines.
Old women exiting tour buses walking to the wall
clutching their purses close to their bodies.
I'm burning incense this morning for your homecoming.
Back from a *conferencia* in which they tried to teach you
all human behavior stems from trauma.
The wasp sting, the nail in my foot, the albino in the woods.
My memory a commemorative plaque
like the clay figurines I keep shelved,
shaped by the hands of my children.
Little colored coiled pots and tea cups
and a crude eggplant-black horse sitting on its haunches
that even Rodin would revere for its roughness.
Like the mud-matted mane of Don Quixote's Rocinante.
And finger marks making public rather than private
the manipulation of material.
If to love is to inhabit.
To carry kerosene and cultivate flowers in the sun
and screen your windows.
Don Quixote subverts his physical senses:

sees festooned pagan warriors battling in a field
where there are only two herds of sheep.
His horse unconcerned with his sanity.
And an unglazed tiny terracotta turtle
with a broken fin and divots
scored onto its carapaced back.
Eyes two unoccupied depressions
likely made with a pencil eraser pressed.

Bent

If love is to be thirsty in the night
un-slaked in the day,
the day without parameters—
or motion detectors monitoring
the way I configure my neck
unruly on the axis of my spine,
the down-turned mouths of many
in the immeasurable heat
petitioning bits of pollen for their throats.
Tell me, how close I can place my hands
up against a man's cage?
How close our veined temples to rock?
There is a statue from ancient Greece of a veiled man—
so as not to be disturbed or diverted
while on a sacred pilgrimage.
Tented in the day,
unguarded in the night,
opening like the five poisonous petals
of a trumpet flower.
Shuddering on the sheath of a mountain.
Eve was bent into being
to allay the isolation of Adam.
Seated behind him on a vintage Indian bike,
she leans her lithe body into each turn,
tugs at her jeans to cover her ass
and sips tequila from a flask.
Neither one wears a helmet.
If love is to be thirsty in the night

un-slaked in the day,
I am bent around the darkness of the sun
siphoning salt from your skin,
eating almonds from your cupboards,
drinking the last of the lake water
as the sails come to a halt on the sand.
I will never give back the lake its love!
It's mine! It's mine! —Loch Ness monster
or man on the shore carving canoe paddles,
I'm not certain. It's so dark without the moon,
difficult to find the far encampment—
the inward holy body.

Christina-the-Astonishing

I want your name.
The fire that burns inside me leaves no discernible marks
and this nausea makes me insane.
I am strapped to a sheetless cot in hell,
seven televisions simultaneously outcrying night and day.
The only food served is white rice, the beverage Coke in a can.
They say you threw yourself into a furnace and reemerged
with no sign of burning upon you, and after one of your seizures
they took you for dead. But after the singing of the Agnus Dei
you arose full of vigor, flew from your coffin and perched like a bird in the rafters.
You are here because I want a playmate and a subject other than self.
My little Bushtit, let me tell you a little about myself: I eat only brown rice,
copulate with only one two-legged creature. *To fuse permanently: bind.*
Let's play a round or two of Truth or Dare.
Yesterday I came home to three nearly identical dead birds,
two in the planter bed with the white butterfly bush, one in the driveway gravel.
And why did I choose you? Because you alighted in the tiniest branches
nourished by milk dripping from your virginal breasts?
An element of homoeroticism, or am I simply saddened that milk
no longer flows from mine? My children appear to love me, perhaps
they'll never put me in a nursing home. The church has kept you out
of the sanctioned canon of saints on the grounds
that you are not the beau ideal to follow, yet many name you
the Patron Saint of Insanity, Mental Disorders, and Psychiatrists.
Some build you a little altar of alder wood and bells.
Truth: you were born a peasant. *One that tills the soil.*
Or, *a rather uneducated uncouth person in the low income group.*
A scamp.

After you and your sisters were orphaned you became a shepherdess.

Yesterday we found a shearer of sheep on Craigslist: $10 per.

Christina, I really want to learn how to be hungryhappily,

how to be at peace with emptiness, how to ride its crest.

I'm not sure how old you were when you really died, but my guess

is that I have already outlived you. That's not necessarily sad, for if you had

lived to my age you would likely have no teeth left in your antiphonal mouth.

At some point you must have tired of those townspeople and their dogs

chasing after you, hogtying—and then dragging you out of the woods.

To make (a thrown animal) helpless.

I have tired of the airport with its canned warnings

not to allow a stranger to coax you into carrying his or her luggage.

The heat of the sun exiling me further into the shade.

Dare: unstrap yourself from the mill's water wheel, let your lame leg

bring you back to the world, I need you.

Even if it's only an epileptic's pity you impart to me—

or an instance of devotion.

Lingual

Scantily clad is the language of beauty
rather than condemning as unfit.
How thin a shirt—
how strong the tongue of the sun.
Hanuman was a celibate monkey
whose single drop of sweat impregnated a fish.
Chrysanthemums and *marigolds*
wrapped around the god's neck.
Objects as symbols to divine the dark:
lockets & lanterns & lead ropes.
Equatorial-necked blue bottles
and field chickweed blistering.
The throat like a snake in the rhythm of rain.
Some of us staying ten feet back from the altar
as if we are made of contaminants.
Others of us enticing the gods
to enter the arena of body,
the atmosphere of soil.
Be-bop-a-lula, she's my baby
is the language of possession.
A relic anklebone wrapped in linen.
How short, or shimmied-up a skirt—
how level a floor.
Some of us banging our wash on rocks.
Letters strung together to sound out a meaning:
hush, harlot, shush, ferret.
In some circles it is a sin
to assign God a lover.

The blow-up doll is mute,
the buffalo grass compliant.
You and I on the back portal, a little drunk,
we saw two unexplainable lights.
I am your mirror, here are the stones
is the language of devotion.
Like the act of the grandmother
who embroidered her grandsons' underwear
with their names & flowers
before bringing them to the orphanage.
And the uncle,
who brought them home
on a donkey.

Down-by-the-River

I took a shit hiding behind skinny oaks
and the blossom-less stalks of horseweed and wood sage.
But I didn't kill anyone.
After only a few days here in the Carolina woods
my hair turning grey at the roots.
Ancestors come from Ireland; you'd think I'd know a song or two
to wail in a bar with lumberjacks buying me lager.
Or a lament to sing with the woman playing the violin.
Some of us like gypsies around the campfire,
and that moon, that moon, that hit of light
like being thrown down a flight of back porch steps,
like touching an electric fence
or bleaching your best girlfriend's
down-her-bony-back black hair
starlight white.
I long for the lightning
of your ejaculate in my mouth, on my breasts,
between the folds and fabric of my flower.
Call it a pussy or a cunt, or the shores of an eel-infested river.
It's so fertile here they drink Pabst right out of the can
and ferns are shedding spores in January.
The only problem I see about relocating to this pasture land
is they baptize each other in shapeless sacks.
And it's still the women who do all the laundering.
The act itself is not demeaning.
Only do not mention spot removers or fabric softeners,
nor speak the sovereign syntax of cultural superiority
pretending to care about the young girls

who open their mouths like milking machines on dairy farms,
or take it in the ass, all to remain immaculate until marriage.
I wiped my ass with dry oak leaves, and yes it scratched.
But I haven't told you anything
that could be admissible as evidence.
I haven't told you anything terribly beautiful.
So I'll tell you about the baby
born nine-fingered under the new moon
behind the pen of unbroken mules.
And about the tree I saw in the Carolina woods—
a huge one hundred year-old blue spruce
that laid down its life to become a footbridge across the river.

Getting Back on the Back of the Horse

The movement is initiated by the dark principle, the feminine,
which advances to meet the light principle, the masculine.
—I Ching

A slow getting back up
having fallen from an invented height,
the ground still frozen
having slumbered in the sedition of seduction,
years of the body in the mirror,
the curve of fat against a hip,
duct of milk splayed on the sofa,
transmigration of moths across the shoulders
unaware of the absence of alfalfa in the nest.
Now one sneakered foot in the stirrup,
the other in the dirt with the dandelions.
The height of the horse's hollowed hide,
like climbing the mountain meadowed
in indigo irises, white yarrow stalks,
a steep ascent over barren boulders.
Hard to rise and mount after hearing the herald
proclaim your poetry too dark.
The messenger subjected to a slaying.
Though seeing more clearly now
the cataracts that concealed the rider
from the holes in her shawl.
The oracle is consulted with the help of yarrow stalks.
Fifty stalks are used for this purpose.
One is put aside and plays no further part.
One must try and survive
the wilderness of one's own backyard,
return with mud on her lips, lipstick on her arms.

Riding rein-less in the circus tent standing
barefooted on the back of the horse cantering
in circles until the canvas flap of the tent lifts
and the sun shines its light into the empty arena
and invites the horse and its rider into the sky:
He comes to meet with his horns.
A melon covered with willow leaves.

In the Yard of the Sanatorium

At nineteen a court gifted me
custody of my fifteen-year-old brother.
I ushered him away from a shattered shop window
to the North in a beat-up light-blue Chevy van
with bald tires, a windowless door, and no heat.

We smoked too much weed, ate balls of seitan
and buttered loaves of homemade whole wheat bread.
Swam in the river, walked in hip-high snow, sketched beech trees
in charcoal, listened to Nick Drake and Dave Van Ronk,
read books about Findhorn and Kahlil Gibran's Jesus.

Today my brother sells recycled carpet,
is getting a divorce. Has a ten-year-old daughter
named for a flower, that he drives
from the Arizona desert to the Pacific Ocean
just to swim in the waves with her.
He does Birkram Yoga in a room of 105 degrees.
At the end is the corpse pose.

In late October of that nineteenth year,
I stripped bare and jumped in the cold water
of the acherontic river. Satan appeared
on a black rock and I stepped on his
torso and on his face—in the service
of remaining sedulous with my self-baptism.

•

I am having difficulty
with this type of narrative,
this curriculum vitae approach.
Too much space between the words
like stalks of corn that never touch
despite the corridor of wind in the rows
and not enough space between the words,
like the suffocation of chickens.

It's as if I am drinking Splenda in decaf wearing sensible shoes
walking in single file to the lavatory to wash my hands.

And these stanzas
like a toddler's building blocks—
primary colors or pale oak?
These simple syntaxed sentences
like oatmeal on the wall.
Salamanders in the yard of the sanatorium.

And will I be shot like Tony Hoagland
in the back out back behind the diner
after eating a hot fudge sundae?
Or was it a slice of rhubarb pie?

All this self-absorption,
like a bleached and pluvial paper towel.
All these accidents of blood, accidents of berries—

utilize the cuff of your cotton sleeve,
the hem of your calico skirt
to mop up the spill.

She Had Some Water

She had some water—
She had some bits of Styrofoam
like white loam, like PVC pipe,
like the teeth of swans swathing the sidewalk near the sea
She had some mesquite honey
She had some coffee that scarred her tongue
She built a dam to cage the water
She reclined on rock in the repose of a reptile,
not unlike when you put your feet up
on the red Formica kitchen table because you're tired
She had a parakeet and clothed it in a cape
to cause an evanescent blindness, a neophilia of night
She had some opal rings
She had some suede shoes
She had some shock and Yerba Mate tea with sugar before sugar was malevolent
She had some cracked clay pots full of marigolds
She had some sweatshirts
She had some aubergine skirts
She had some pollywogs
She had some cranberry juice
She had some sebaceous cysts but no sisters
to bail the water out of the leaky rowboat
the summer she was under the spell of skunks
She had a hawk pendant
She had a hammer
She had two children coifed in the habiliments of harbor seals for Halloween
She had some stomach cramps
She had some radiant heaters

She had some hoses where there should have been chrome
She occluded the water to fence it as her own
She had some adipose tissue
She had some red Jell-O
She had some eye contact with big horn sheep and
caliginous strangers in passing cars
She had some rats she tried to poison
She had some dumbbells and declensions
She had some galumptious moments, hours, days
She had some sun ascertaining ownership on her shoulders
She had some rain in her hair
She had some *disjecta membra* of memory of being in a lion's lair
of being in a supply closet
of being unpolished.

Alchemy

I once told you I like the smell of owl dung
drying in the leaves under the cottonwood trees.

On the trail along the railroad tracks
we watched the male mount the female in the dusk.

Sometimes I see things. In Jerez, in the Gypsy Barrio,
an infant pacifier lying disembodied in a dark and rain-wet alley.

In Tulum, a tulip hanging from a hook & a one-armed boy asleep
in the shade of a broken wall. My son says I am not a mother.

Jung said *nigredo* is the moment of maximum despair.
We have all held up crosses, cowering like the crawling man

in Dali's *The Temptation of St. Antonius,*
but not all of us have been gifted with the erotica of answers.

I like the smell of composting soil,
black as the tongue of a giraffe.

The mouth is not the lips, or the tongue—
but the entrance and the exit.

Albedo, the light of interrogation lamps,
the cerement halos of cinder blocks.

•

There is beauty in the graffiti etched on the cathedral wall,
beauty in the body of the owl my son and I buried.

I'm as afraid of dying as anyone.
I don't want to die the death of Anna Karenina.

Sometimes I don't see things and trample over pollinating flowers.
Rubedo is the blood in the stamens—

the narcotic curve of a cherry bomb,
the two star rubies

you carried out into the sun to let me lose myself a little
in their resurrecting light.

Spinning

Another morning of snow, and of a son
who does not speak to me
because my lover is not his father.
I broom the white weight from my car windows.
Drive to the gym for spin class
where nine other storm-wet women
find reprieve in the rhythms and beats
of the Blues and Afro-Cuban pop
by pumping our legs on stationary bikes.
We sweat and sway as if we are
on the dense-bodied dance floors
of Tennessee roadhouses, NYC discos,
New Orleans Blues bars and red-stained barns.
Barns where calves and colts are birthed,
where rusted tractor parts lie collapsed in a corner,
where on a Saturday night a black-walnut banjo,
a waxed fiddle, and an acoustic guitar
make lovers out of the ordinary and the deaf.
My son nearly mute.
His only words: *Get away from me.*
If I could come clean I would tell him
that his pain is my making.
Our children delivered to us
by negligent gods and large-backed birds—
nearly flawless in body and soul
until we drop, nick, and chip them.
And sometimes worse things are done to their bodies
in circumstances beyond us.

The woman on the bike next to me
is the thinnest and always cold.
She keeps a beach towel wrapped around her
while the rest of us shed layers.
She watches our bodies to tell hers how to move.
But this morning, when Muddy Waters sang about lust,
and again when Al Green crooned about love,
I heard her howl a little hoot,
like a convalescing animal in a cardboard box.
I drove home unhurriedly on the icy road,
passed my son in his old cop car on his way late to school.
He lifted two fingers from his left hand
ever so slightly from the steering wheel
in acknowledgment.
I was grateful that he was still moving—
even if in a direction away from me.

Mechanical Bull

I have never wanted for much.
Never once wished
to be a barrel racer, or a rodeo queen.
I share the same birthday as the Mexican poet
Rosario Castellanos who died
from *an unfortunate electrical accident.*
Though I did just see my first mechanical bull
in a bar. A black velvet-skinned beast
the girth of a downed tree,
saddle-less and horned—
Guernica, and Gumby, and gallant.
I was tempted to go in and ride it, but R. said
don't even think of it in that short dress.
And that made me think of it more.
He used to like to shake his head and say *you're O.D.D.*
which stands for oppositional defiant disorder.
Recently he informed me that label/diagnosis is only for children
and I became sad. I was somewhat proud to be O.D.D.
Not realizing that it spelled *odd,*
whose number one definition in the dictionary
given to me by the daughter of its previous owner
who no longer worships words because she has Alzheimer's
and has been moved into a place called Rainbow Vision—
is that which is without its corresponding mate:
that lacks its complimentary match.
They say Cezanne painted the way he did because of his failing eyesight.
More likely he had his own variety of oppositional defiant disorder.
One amassed of rooftops and hues of horizontals dismantled.

Could it be that I have located my other sock?
Rosario asked *What have we come here for, night,
heart of night? / Dream that we do not die. / And,
at times, for a moment, wake.* I was once struck
by lightning, but that is a lie. Though I keep
grabbing hold of electric fences. She also wrote
We kill what we love, what's left / Was never alive.
It is only down at the bottom—the final entry
that reads: *nonconforming in behavior.*

Please, Come In

Shaking and shivering, just the right fit of trembling.
The wind is thrashing its spotted wings
against the weakening walls of my house
seeking to slip into caulked cracks
and knock me down, my head against brick
or the stainless steel of a trash compactor.
There is elk blood in my refrigerator
dripping from white butcher paper.
One man's vision of seduction—
as if a piercing with arrows into the throat
or heart of a beast can load one's soul with love.
Outside my front door there's a hole
like a small moon crater once meant to house a pond
with sun-glistening carp and succulently fat lilies
like the ones in the muted pastels of Monet.
I've heard it is hell to be in love with a painter—
better to be in love with the paint.
Blue pigments powdered by the pounding of stones;
Venetian red raked from the breast of a lake bird.
Iron oxides rusting into the purple-black of sugared figs.
I hate it when I hand a dollar to homeless man
and he says "*God bless you.*"
There's a torn and crooked trampoline
out the backdoor of my house,
we lie on it anyway and look to the night sky.
Neither one of us knows the nomenclature of stars.
Neither one of us knows how to leave the night.
There are explosives in barrels in the garage

and three broken-rung ladders,
a red vinyl punching bag and an out-of-tune piano.
There's an axe and an ice-making machine
and an empty doll cradle.
I use the axe to chop kindling,
it is getting so cold.

Snow

If snow is a gift,
why not wrap ourselves in its hollow drifts?
Furrow under as if we are snowshoe hares
or beavers whose waters are frozen.
Why not wear the mask of beauty
until the angel takes it away
and tosses it into the pile at the gate?
A man with a shovel in his hand
is a sexy thing.
I dare myself to bury my dead,
to incline towards Cupid's clouds.
I dare myself to love a man all-out.
I'm less afraid of the stray hairs of strangers
left behind in hotel bathtubs;
less afraid of the sounds in the wind.
Conversing is sometimes useless,
like beavers clawing ice—
hoping to erase back into water.
There is never one millisecond of nothingness.
Someone is always nodding their head.
Some tractor is always taking out a tree.
Some child is always spilling a glass of juice.
I hate talking to you on the phone.
I can't touch your hair, or bite your neck.
Too many in-between places to hide.
Someone is always looking for a lost necklace.
Someone is always crying in a confessional.
Some form of Satan always creating static

to interrupt the songs.
You told me after everyone left
you stayed behind
and shoveled dirt over your father.
When we walked in the snow
I told you that I longed to be under
the current of the creek—
to be more hushed, less human.
Still, there are no sins between us,
only scratches on river-scented skin,
tufts of goat hair in the wind.

May 25

Women have always inserted objects into orifices.
Swan feathers are offered to pacify the sea.
I once refused a gift of a sex toy.
The original rosary was 165 rolled rose petals.
Think of the hands doing such affectionate work.
My birth on May 25 makes me a twin:
one of me immobile on the mattress,
the other never leaves the mountain.
Women have always inserted objects into orifices:
oiled snakes and molted stones;
sphinx moths and cygnet eggs.
After the execution of Christ
Mary Jacobe and Mary Salome
were banished to the sea without food, water,
or sails. Black Sara, queen of the gypsies,
swam out and rescued them.
Every May 25 statues of Sara and the two Marys
are taken out of wax-sealed crates
from the crypt of *Les Saintes-Maries-de-la-Mer*
and carried onto a boat to bless the sea.
Women have always inserted objects into orifices:
the tongue of a panther, the fist of a fox.
The juice of wild poppies drunk as anesthetic.
There are days when I can't get out of bed:
languor and legs weaving anamnesis and appetite.
Days when I can't get wet, afraid of water.
So much is decided by the timbre of the sky,
by the particles afloat in our blood.

Somniloquy and the distillation of rose water.
The tongue extends itself to lilt on one's own nipple,
blessed by the visitation of pigeons on the lintel.
Hands tying white sheets to make a ladder;
hands unraveling the twine of a torn kite
toward the sky.

Closer to the Surface

Withdrawing from the world,
letting go the coralline-crusted
anchor from the ocean floor—
as if a detached retina might help
one see the face of God or a ghost.
My son left, to enter the world,
with thirty pounds on his young back.
The house still holds his scent.
I am reading about renunciation
of the flesh, *contemptus mundi*,
and ascetics fainting in frigid waters.
Benedict of Aniane let lice live on his skin.
St. Teresa said *Love proves itself by deeds.*
I put a knife in my son's toiletry bag,
gave him a ride to the airport.
She scattered flowers.
Safecrackers sandpaper their fingertips
so touch receptors will be closer to the surface.
The skin a salve, a veil, a cloak—
an embellished fragment, an atmosphere.
St. John of the Desert stood for three years
against a silica-striated rock in prayer
without once succumbing to the lure of gravity
until his feet split and putrefied, and
"an angel appeared . . . and made him leave that place."
My son left with one pair of shitty thin-soled sneakers
and walked in the mountains of Morocco
until he twisted his ankle from a fall and it frightened him.

A burro carried him for a day.

How overrated civilization is.

How carnal the faith of the innocent:

a tin cup and a tarp—

how beautiful the blue accordion.

The day before he left my son pointed to a hawk in the sky.

Bull's-eye

There used to be beautiful cows grazing outside my window.
Primordial and feral like the ones we maneuver around
on the aspen trail in the mountains.
The ones I am afraid of.
Their opaque eyes; my feet in mud.
My man shields me from the beasts
with his body. I don't want him addressing
another woman as *Beautiful.*
Sitting next to her at a bar, nor typed in an email,
so he calls me high-strung.
William Burroughs killed his wife
playing William Tell drunk.
He missed the apple on her head.
And no scientist or clairvoyant has been able to zero-in
on the centers of sexuality in the human brain.
As if to mark the map with little flags,
as if to go to market without your recyclable bag.
As a child I shot a bow and arrow
into a hay bale in a high meadow.
Taut then slack,
Miss Mary Mack . . . all down her back. . . .
Now behind the barbed wire fence
trees named *Pinion* and *Juniper,*
Cholla cactus. Two days ago
two teenage girls galloping on horses.
In the dark tunnel of night my man calls me his *Vida.*
There is the belief by some forest dwelling tribe
that a woman's womb is both birth canal and coffin.

Neruda's mother died two months after giving birth to him.
From complications, or from falling down the stairs—
I don't know. My mother and I forced
into communion by overlapping skin.
I was born without a doctor.
I will die without a doctor.
Someone will eye me behind the fence
and be afraid of a woman walking away.
Zeroing-out rather than in.

No Identity Crisis Here

There is a woman named J. Dominique
who barely accepts the fact of being a woman.
And in some circles, or centuries, she would be seen
as an old-woman. Or an adulteress. Or a nun
of no particular propensity for sainthood.
Not because she's ever believed she was a male among men,
but because last she looked she was a girl without blood.
No, she has never suffered
from penis envy, although she is grateful for
and shows off her boyishly small hips
and faint blond mustache.
And where was it that she first heard
The Irish are the Mexicans of the British Isles?
How J. Dominique longs to be canonized
or at least have her portrait painted on some barrio wall
or Celtic ruin where flowers and love notes
will be left after her passing and candles lit
until the monsoons of June extinguish the flames
and her lover who has sworn
that after her there will be no other
is hankering after the ass of a woman in a snake-hemmed skirt
who is selling stolen flowers from J. Dominique's shrine.
Canonized or not, the stories will circulate after her death:
With one touch of her hand
upon the mournful lap of a man wanting to be a woman
his penis vanished into the a priori world
of genital warehouses and sultry tent cabarets.
A place where Country Western women

and Qawwali singing men can lay down together
in the mud without shame or sore throats
and seek transmutations of skin and God and sorrow
and climax on go-cart tracks shaped like
the over-sized earrings of women at their second weddings.
J. Dominique is certain that Christ will return soon
for his slugabed Second Coming
as a guest at the wedding of two men madly in love
and turn tap water into bubbly water,
World Wrestling Federation wrestlers into herring,
and toothpicks into torches.
This time around he may be a diamond appraiser
or a man eating grits in a diner.
He may be a woman in a Detroit Pistons jersey
shaving her legs under a campground spigot.
Or a hunter hiding from a helicopter
bedded down in cord grass.
But J. Dominique will have no trouble
recognizing him by his alkaline scent
and that saint-of-all-saints look in his eyes
as if he resides elsewhere.
And she'll be ashamed for her ego-driven desire
to be listed among the holy,
and humbled into a hallow love for her body—
no matter how temporary the occupancy.

Acknowledgments

I would like to thank Tony Hoagland and Dana Levin, whose support and generosity has been boundless.

I would like to thank Elizabeth Scanlon, Ellen Dore Watson, and Dean Young.

I would like to thank Sarah Gorham and all of the staff at Sarabande Books.

I would like to thank the Rona Jaffe Foundation.

I would like to thank all the unnamed poets, family members, and friends who have added wildness and shelter to my imaginative life.

I would like to acknowledge that without Anselmo Ronald Gallegos there would be no love poems in this collection.

Grateful acknowledgment is given to the editors of the publications in which the following poems first appeared:

The American Poetry Review: "A Down-by-the-River Poem," "Alchemy," "Animal Love," "Ars Poetica, Or Keeper-of-the-Water," "Bears and Marmots," "Bent," "Christina-the-Astonishing," "Closer to the Surface," "Coat-of-Arms," "Feral Fields," "Harem," "Kyphosis," "Late Night Confessions," "Lingual," "The Skin of an Otter," "May 25," "Mechanical Bull," "No Identity Crisis Here," "Possession," and "Supine in the Sun in the Neighborhood of Naked"

The Cortland Review: "Wedded to Dirt" (as "Love Poem: flat out")

Conduit: "Absolution" and "Snow"

FIELD: "Please, Come In" and "Surrender"

Longshot: "Under House Arrest"

The Massachusetts Review: "In the Geometry of Less" and "Bull's-eye"

The New England Review: "Discalced," "Photuris P.," and "The Relativity of Sorrows"

POETRY: "Beaded Baby"

The Queen City Review: "Request to a Lover"

The Spoon River Poetry Review: "Bareback"

TriQuarterly: "Spinning"

Following a brief foray into the slam and performance poetry world, **Joanne Dominique Dwyer** went on to study at the College of Santa Fe where she received a BA in Creative Writing. She earned her MFA from Warren Wilson College in 2009. Dwyer is a recipient of a Rona Jaffe Foundation Writers' Award, a Bread Loaf Scholar award, and the Anne Halley Poetry Prize. Her poems have appeared in *The American Poetry Review, Conduit, FIELD, Many Mountains Moving, The Massachusetts Review, New England Review, POETRY, Spoon River Poetry Review, TriQuarterly,* and other magazines. Currently, she resides in Northern New Mexico and works as facilitator for the Alzheimer's Poetry Project.